SAGUARO

A VIEW OF
SAGUARO
NATIONAL
MONUMENT
& THE
TUCSON BASIN

text by Gary Paul Nabhan

photography by George H.H. Huey

SOUTHWEST PARKS AND
MONUMENTS ASSOCIATION
Tucson, Arizona

ACKNOWLEDGMENTS

The paper for printing this publication, and in part the idea for it, have been contributed by the Mohawk Paper Company. We particularly thank Scott Petrequin for his interest in this collaboration. We also thank Robert Arnberger, Ed Pilley, Jane Cole, Karen Reichhardt, Janice Bowers, Steven McLaughlin, Julie Dreher, Susan Wells, Richard Hayes, Jim Jarchow, Frank Reichenbacher, Kevin Dahl, Michael Collier, Clay May, Peter Warshall, Patricia Paylore and Arizona-Sonora Desert Museum staff for reading earlier drafts of this manuscript, or providing help in obtaining information and photos. Additionally, Nabhan wishes to express his gratitude to four ''desert women:'' Karen Reichhardt for joining in these explorations; Janice Bowers, for sharing unpublished manuscripts and other insights regarding the Rincons; Jerri Nabhan, for holding down the fort (kids) during some of the field work; and Pat Paylore, for providing inspiration, bibliographic assistance and editorial blessings.

SAGUARO by Gary Paul Nabhan
Copyright 1986 by Southwest Parks
& Monuments Association
ISBN 0-911408-69-X
Library of Congress Number 86-061422
Editing: T.J. Priehs
Copy Editing: Carolyn Dodson
Design: Christina Watkins
Production: Christina Watkins,
T.J. Priehs, Robert Petersen

SAGUARO was printed on Mohawk Superfine soft white, 80# text & cover, Poseidon 80#, and Ticonderoga, peach, 70#
typeset in Trump Midiaeval with Eurostile by Typesmith, Inc., Tucson, Arizona
color separations by VisiColor, Inc., Denver, Colorado
lithographed by Lorraine Press, Salt Lake City, Utah

Frontispiece: ''Cereus Giganteus'' from the Emory *Report on the United States & Mexican Boundary Survey,* 1848.
Courtesy the Desert Botanic Gardens library.
Title page: saguaro forest
Contents: white-winged dove, saguaro fruit
Page 6: Tanque Verde Ridge, light snow

CONTENTS

THE
LONG-LIVED
GIANT
& THE
EPHEMERAL
BELLYFLOWER

"Coming down the northern point of the (Rincon) mountain and out westward into the plain, we transferred ourselves in a few hours from the temperate to the torrid zone. In the foot-slopes we passed through an ardent grove of giant cacti, called by the Mexicans 'Sahuaros,' some of them fifty feet high. Among these prickly horrors grew a variety of lesser ones . . ."

Lt. John Bigelow, Jr., 1887

IT IS THE TIME OF YEAR when the weather takes its first turn from mild towards torrid, when most animals, humans included, begin ducking into shade during the midday heat. For whatever reason it may be, you have found yourself out in the cactus forest at noon, feeling a little like a fish in a tree. You are not far from cover, your head is well-shaded by an old straw sombrero, and a canteen is on your hip, but nonetheless the increasing heat and drought here command your respect. These are conditions for the hardy, and the life that endures here embodies a tough kind of beauty.

For the moment, however, you are hydrated enough to walk amidst the tall, columnar cacti just now breaking into bud. You feel dwarfed by these giants, overwhelmed by their stature. The soon-to-bloom saguaros you see are all taller than you are, seven feet up to nearly forty feet in this stand.

The green weight held within a mature saguaro's fluted flanks ranges from seventy-five to ninety-five percent water. Even when it is so dry that cactus roots can no longer extract moisture from the soil, these living towers keep enough water in their photosynthetic tissue to continue their food-making activities. During the coming dry months, their diameters will shrink and fold in like an accordion. Their ribs become more angled as water is lost from their storage cells in order to maintain that needed by their photosynthetic machinery. Young saguaros have been known to endure an 80 percent water loss from their stems during drought, without dying. In contrast, desert scientist Schmidt-Nielson reminds us that "a man is physically and mentally unable to take care of himself at ten

saguaro blossom

percent weight loss (due to depletion of fluids), and at about twelve percent water deficit he is unable to swallow and can no longer recover without assistance."

Even saguaros which achieve maximum heights above forty feet obtain all their water from root systems which seldom sink deeper than three feet into the earth. However shallow, these roots can extend laterally from the base of the plant for as much as 100 feet—twice as far as the tallest saguaro reaches into the sky. So close to the ground surface, they can rapidly respond to the slightest of rains, drawing in enough water to maintain a moisture supply of one to several tons in mature saguaros.

Perhaps in addition to feeling dwarfed, you feel humbled. These lumbering giants, ten to thirty times heavier than you are, can endure conditions that will make you wither and wane. They need no canteens like the one artificially implanted on your hip. You learn, too, that they eclipse you in longevity—the forty-footer not far from you may be 150 years in age, born before Arizona was part of the United States!

One particular plant, Mexican by birth, was not even a half foot tall when George Engelmann first scientifically described the species as *Cereus giganteus* in 1848. During the winter of that same year, many young saguaros situated in exposed sites were killed when a historically unprece-dented snowstorm left three-foot drifts on the desert floor, covering plants with snow for several days. The juvenile saguaros that were sheltered by tree canopies and by the partial cover of rocks were among the few survivors of this catastrophic freeze. Others, badly damaged, became especially susceptible to infection. They rotted and fell over, leaving ghostly silhouettes of themselves decaying on the ground. Because it was sheltered beneath a nurse plant—a tree such as palo verdo or mesquite which buffers its underlings from extreme temperatures—this particular saguaro suffered only a minor freeze scar at its base.

Five years and another six inches of growth later, the United States negotiated the Gadsden purchase with the Mexican government, and took over all the lands between the Gila River and the present-day international boundary. This saguaro, still under cover beneath its palo verde, became a U.S. citizen. By the time Lieutenant Bigelow came over the Rincon Mountains to first describe the cactus stand within what is now Saguaro National Monument, the plant was ten feet tall and producing delicious red fruit.

Bigelow, Crook and other military men had come to Arizona Territory to terminate Apache raids on the sparsely-settled Tucson Basin. As fears of Apaches subsided, O'odham Indians resumed their traditional harvest of saguaro fruit on the rocky bajadas

prickly pear & saguaro

11

rimming the basin, and Mexican-American families built wood-fired kilns to make quicklime near the base of the Rincon Mountains. More Anglo-Americans also moved into the Tucson Basin, many of them to ranch.

These latter activities may have reduced the number of saguaros that could establish themselves on the bajada slopes skirting the Rincons. The number of cattle in Pima County increased dramatically from the late 1870s to about 114,000 head in 1890. Cattle grazed and trampled vegetation that would have otherwise protected young saguaros. Anglo ranchers cut mesquite for cooking fires and for corrals. Mexican-Americans consumed tremendous amounts of palo verde and mesquite to process local limestone in kilns to make the quicklime needed at nearby Fort Lowell. These activities had the collective effect of depleting the nurse plants which would otherwise provide protective cover for young saguaros. By the time a three-year drought hit in the early 1890s, saguaro establishment was on the decline.

The older, Mexican-born saguaro—already over a half century in age—survived the drought. Its water storage tissues and its highly

competitive root system captured much of the sparse rainwater which soaked into the soil around it. This saguaro's nurse plant was not so lucky. Because its roots were deeper than those of the saguaro, it was outcompeted for the little rain which entered the soil, and it died of thirst. In essence, it was killed by the cactus it had nursed along for over sixty years.

From then on, this saguaro put more and more of its energy into reproductive growth, loading on dozens of fruit during June and July, each with a couple thousand seeds inside. When Arizona became a state in 1912, the plant was over twenty feet in height, and had grown arms which enable fruit production to multiply, since each branch bears its own bounty at the tip. By the time Saguaro National Monument was established in 1933, this single saguaro had produced on the order of forty million seeds. Undiminished by periodic drought years, it has continued to bear fruit with millions of more seeds for over another half century.

You look up to the towering saguaro, its bristly spines worn off its ancient flanks, and crusty "boots" for nest holes cored into its arms by woodpeckers. You try juggling the details of its history in your head, but they all tumble down to one notion.

Because its lifespan stretches beyond yours, its full life is beyond your knowing.

Few people have had the perseverance to follow a single saguaro from germination through first flowering some thirty years later, let alone track one plant for longer than that. Who has the tenacity to hang on to one of the *hombres* all the way around its life cycle, on the rocky ride from sprouting seed back to dropping fruit, rotting tissue and dried-out ribs? How many humans have had the patience to know even one saguaro well? And what would it take to get a sense of the sweep of history of a whole forest full of them?

You shake your head sadly. We seem too short-sighted, too *mortal* to be able to comprehend saguaro forests spanning the centuries. Better to focus on something *small*. Your vision glances off the towering trunk of one of these giants; and falls to the ground. And, for the first time, you catch sight of a dash of color at the foot of a nearby saguaro.

It is as alive as the giant cactus, but a hundred times smaller. It weighs perhaps a hundred thousandth of what the saguaro weighs, and its lifespan can be counted in days, not centuries. It seems understandable on your scale of time.

A bellyflower: a blooming plant so small that botanists are inclined to lie on their bellies, examining it with a hand lens, in order to identify it.

More properly, it is called an *ephemeralized* annual herb. Its telescoped life cycle fits within a few months or even weeks between droughts.

Compared to the lanky saguaro, it is an abbreviation. It is germinated with the early winter rains, and lays on the ground as an inconspicuous rosette of finely-divided leaves. Within about six weeks, it has sent up a shoot and has begun to advertise delicate-hued flowers.

Until late spring drought sets in, this miniature will continue to bloom, attracting solitary bees, and throwing off rapidly-setting seeds. Then, as quickly as it sprouted, it will wither and die as the ground dries. It will leave hardly any trace of itself except for the few tiny seeds now dormant in the soil.

Drought casts its mark especially where plants cluster together. A plant found alone in a suitably moist site is less vulnerable to an unpredictable climate than are full-fledged wildflower populations. Of the millions of wildflower seeds lying dormant within your reach, only a relative few will germinate to cloak the desert floor like a living gray-green carpet. Past a point, however, rain or no rain, the rest remain in place, as seed. Desert wildflowers "never put all their eggs in one basket," but why? What's the disadvantage to all of them jumping out of the soil and trying to grow at the same time?

left, uprooted saguaro

Not far from the Tucson Mountains, in the Silverbells, ecologist Richard Inouye found the answer: competition for water. No matter whether you are a bellyflower, a saguaro, or a human, if your population fills up an environment where water is sometimes scarce, sooner or later someone is going to be severely limited.

Where desert wildflower population densities stay relatively low, a higher percentage of individuals survived. They average greater weights per plant and probably produce more seeds per plant than in dense stands. Where competition for water had limited the soil moisture available to each plant, they suffer.

Bellyflowers have worked out a way to keep most of their species from dying of thirst. They delay further germination once a sizeable cover of wildflowers becomes established. A sufficient number of seeds remain in the soil reserve. This keeps the entire population from being devastated in fluke years when a good early rain is followed by a long drought or harsh temperatures.

Moreover, miniscule wildflower seeds can stay "asleep" in desert soils for as much as two centuries. Then, when conditions fit, they awaken to a receptive world.

You feel inclined to move earthward, to take a better look at this self-regulating population, a patch of wildflowers small enough to fit in the joined palms of your hands. But bellyflowers are not the only plants hidden beneath the giant cacti and desert shrubs. Just where you were about to lie down, a tiny saguaro emerges, thorns arched upward as if to deter any creature that presses in too closely....

Other forces will press in on a young saguaro that germinates in open terrain. Saguaro sprouts have an average life expectancy of fewer than six weeks. The more exposed their place of germination, the greater the chance that they will live no longer than the bellyflower.

You stand up, and and your head reels in the noon heat. Your ears sing with the drone of chanting cicadas. It dawns on you that most saguaros are as temporary on the face of the earth as are the ephemeral wildflowers. And though only one in millions of saguaro seeds grows into a giant of a hundred or more years, many wildflower seeds also survive in desert soils that long.

Perhaps what we fail to see at work in the saguaro lifespan, we can see by analogy in the bellyflower. In the long run, survival in a harsh environment is as much influenced by your relationships with neighbors as it is by your own physiological hardiness. Seldom does a single drought season endanger the solitary saguaro, the lone palo verde, or the scatter of small desert wildflowers. Instead, where plants congregate, where resources become too scarce to go around, their numbers are inevitably thinned.

You are ready to head down from the saguaro stand, into the silty flats which were once covered with creosote bushes. The rapidly-growing city of Tucson spans these flats today. In the year that saguaros were scientifically described, Tucson had a population of fewer than 1,000 people. If you lived in Tucson before the Civil War, you would have been outnumbered by saguaros. In the mid-1980s, urban residents number well over 400,000 in the Tucson Basin, and may in fact outnumber the wild saguaros left within the city limits.

It has been argued that *water* will soon become an external control on our population growth, just as it may have become for the prehistoric Hohokam who inhabited the Tucson Basin.

We might do well to consider additional reasons for controlling our own growth. Depending on what we want out of life, we may have to develop our own internal, cultural controls to insure a diverse desert community. You may be asked what you are willing to give up or contribute to live in one kind of desert neighborhood or an-

other. Does it matter to you whether all your neighbors are humans, or do you want room for saguaros too? That you and your different kinds of potential neighbors consume resources at different rates cannot be denied. While a seventy-five year old saguaro con-

sumes about a thousand quarts of water each year, the average human resident in Tucson today uses roughly 250 times that volume. ■

desert tortoise eating prickly pear fruit

spring snow

Drought and freezes. The double punches pounding Sonoran Desert life into shape. Yet these environmental stresses may not always be responsible for the knockouts. Perhaps more often than recognized, rough weather predisposes plants to injury, but other organisims bring them down to the killing floor.

Near the northern limits of saguaro-palo verde forests, climate, competition and bacterial rotting interact in complex ways. These interactions are not merely of academic interest—they have caused concern and consternation in tens of thousands of visitors to Saguaro National Monument over the decades since its establishment. What you see on the Cactus Forest Drive in Saguaro East is vastly different than what visitors viewed there a half century ago. The catastrophic drop in saguaro numbers there has been the subject of a raging scientific debate for decades. It is a controversy that is not yet fully resolved.

Imagine, if you will, that you dreamed of setting up a reserve for saguaros, located in the densest stand you could find. Your dream came true, but soon afterwards the magnificent old cacti within the stand began to dwindle in numbers. It seemed as if the proliferation of young saguaros was not keeping astride with the passing away of elders. The cactus monument was losing the very thing it was set up to preserve.

This very dilemma was what nature lovers in the Tucson Basin faced for several decades following 1939, when it looked as though the Cactus Forest in Saguaro East might cease to exist. The research and management policy of the National Park Service has evolved through the years to accommodate new perspectives and information regarding the biology of key organisms found within parks, and the saguaro story is a classic example of this dynamism.

In the late Twenties, the world-famous ecologist, Homer Shantz, encouraged the state of Arizona to purchase a large reserve on the east side of the Tucson Basin where dense, majestic saguaros inspired scientists and tourists alike. As president of the University of Arizona, Dr. Shantz had in mind using the reserve both for ecological studies and for the location of a university astronomical observatory. When the Great Depression hit, the state was no longer able to make payments on the designated land, and the federal government was asked to purchase and manage the Cactus Forest and its surroundings. In 1933, Saguaro National Monument was officially established, and the Cactus Forest was assured some measure of perpetuity, or so it seemed.

Then, in 1939 came the coldest February on record for Tucson. Both wild and cultivated plants in the Tucson Basin were severely damaged as they suffered several hours of temperatures as low as 25°F. Within a few months, plant pathologists coincidentally discovered a new species of soft rot bacteria infecting local saguaros.

The 1939 freeze may have injured saguaros in a way that predisposed them to rapid infection by this bacterium. Pathologists, however, simply viewed the soft rot as a disease that was rapidly spreading through the Cactus Forest. In 1941, they recommended to the National Park Service that "sanitation" and "surgery" be attempted to remove any arms or whole plants showing symptoms of the disease, since they might serve in spreading the infection to other plants.

This was done. Any rotting saguaros or infected arms found within a half mile of the Cactus Forest were removed and bulldozed into large pits for burial.

Although it was hoped that this act alone would slow mortality in the Cactus Forest, its population continued to dwindle. If a soft rot carried by wide-ranging insects was truly ravaging the Cactus Forest, then a sanitation program capable of saving it would need to be enormous. Some of the pathologists despaired. The public worried that saguaros might "eventually disappear . . . [creating] a tragedy no less saddening that would the extermination of the giant redwoods." In the late Fifties and early Sixties, the Park Service entertained propagating saguaros in lath house nurseries, for future transplanting into the Cactus Forest. This would be done to keep Cactus Forest densities from slipping any further.

Meanwhile, other scientists began noticing a high correlation of the rot with drought stress, wounds and other injuries. Older plants appeared unable to fend off the rot by building a bootlike callus to exclude it from internal tissues. It seemed that susceptible plants would rot and die no matter what. The artificial replenishment of saguaro populations could not, in and of itself, stop that trend.

About the same time, policy within the National Park Service opened toward another direction, that of more passive acceptance of plant and animal population fluxes. The Park Service should no longer intervene in nature's dynamics, if it could be shown that temporal variations in mortality were natural events.

Enter two ecologists: Dr. Charles Lowe, already well-established in desert biology, and Warren "Scotty" Steenbergh, a Lowe student who would devote the next two decades of his life to the saguaro story. To piece together the story, Steenbergh led a team in crawling over acres of desert to find miniscule saguaro seedlings. They climbed up ladders during the peak heat of the summer to probe the flowers, fruit, boots and tissue of the remaining old giants. Lowe sought to relate the sweep of saguaro density fluxes to broad climatic patterns, as well as to the particular amounts of solar radiation reaching saguaro seedlings in their microenvironments.

They concluded that the dense Cactus Forest for which Saguaro National Monument was established existed as a short term phenomenon. It was a mere ephemeral bloom on the evolutionary time scale. Catastrophic freezes of twenty hours or more in duration may happen decades apart, but they were key in thinning out old saguaros. Particularly at the upper, northeast edge of the saguaro's range, these freezes sporadically reshaped the spectrum of ages that could be found within a cactus forest.

With *the* Cactus Forest in particular, it had been spared severe frosts for several decades prior to 1939, and its members had grown old and tall. When the 1939 freeze came, cataclysmic thinning was inevitable. Steenbergh and Lowe saw bacterial infection not as a disease which spread through the population, but as the decay of tissue already damaged or killed by freezing temperatures.

Philosophically, they felt that the Cactus Forest "demise" was only a problem if considered in terms of the human life span. The "solution" to such a problem was not the expensive artificial regeneration of saguaros to please the monument's visitors. Instead, they suggested, we all must adopt the longer-term "perspective offered by the time scale of evolution."

Thanks to the establishment of Saguaro West in the Tucson Mountains in the early 1960s, park visitors now have the opportunity to view another large cactus population at a different stage in its natural fluctuations. By contrasting the higher-elevation stand in Saguaro East with that seen along the drive through Saguaro West, it

bulldozing saguaro for burial, 1941

is possible to gain a sense of saguaros in the context of this deeper time scale.

While Lowe's and Steenbergh's saguaro studies are both instructive and eloquent, they historically represented a swing on the pendulum away from preoccupation with soft rot as a disease within saguaro populations. Perhaps the pendulum is swinging back to further consider bacteria's place in saguaro ecology. A fascinating story has emerged that includes not only bacteria, but yeasts and fruit flies, and their ties to saguaros.

Dr. Stanley Alcorn and his assistant Tom Orum have identified several groups of *Erwinia* bacteria that can be found in rotting tissues of cacti. Some appear to be introductions spread from cultivated crops, a common substrate for *Erwinia* worldwide. However, one large group known as the "cactus soft-rotters" appears to be native, and highly associated with saguaro, prickly pear, cholla and barrel cactus.

Insects, birds and violent dust storms are suspected as carrying these bacteria into saguaro wounds, for such bacteria cannot on their own breach these cacti's armor. Once established, they multiply and produce enzymes that break down cactus cells into nutrients that the bacteria then absorb. If, however, the bacteria are somehow introduced into a healthy, non-stressed plant, the cactus seals off the infected pocket of tissue by forming a callus around it, much like that of a crusty saguaro boot. The bacteria can then spread no further into the plant's tissues.

When stressed by freezes, prolonged drought, root damage, herbicides, waterlogging or senility, saguaros apparently lose their ability to internally control the bacteria. Dr. Alcorn has seen soft rot affect saguaros of all ages, from frost-free to freeze-stricken zones. The stressed host plant can ward off infection only to a point. A deep puncture wound, a critical mass of bacteria or severe stress will tip the balance toward the rot. Once this balance is disrupted, the microorganisms rapidly overpower their grandiose host. A Goliath is toppled and returned to earth.

The story does not stop there, for the soft rot produces a volatile chemical which attracts fruit flies that have evolved to take advantage of cactus wounds. The fruit flies carry a yeast that further speeds the decay of the fallen saguaro. Saguaro fruit flies lay their eggs in the pockets of rot, and their larvae feed upon the by-products of the yeast. Ecologists now believe that each group of cacti—organpipes, prickly pears, saguaros and others—maintains its own specific community of yeasts and fruit flies. Since bacteria are the key link in these co-evolved communities, it is unlikely that such a complex system could have evolved if the *Erwinia* had been recently introduced from agricultural crops.

Bacteria—we usually think of them only in relation to our own wounds. Yeasts—the magical microbes responsible for beer and bread. Fruit flies—we seldom see them unless we spot them on bruised peaches and pears. Special sets of these organisms could not now exist were it not for rewards they reap from stressed saguaros.

BEDROCK MORTARS, CONTOURED TERRACES & THE UNDERLYING CHAOS

"Each boulder encapsulates the story of the mountain—in the mineral crystals which give each its texture, in the events which raised to this lofty altitude the layers from which each boulder was weathered. . . . On this journey continents rift apart, crash together, and drift about the planet. . . . Somehow a single piece of granite will survive eons of these cosmic forces to absorb solar heat . . . and transmit it to the chilled skin of an individual member of a recently evolved mammalian species. No survival could be more moving."

Stephen Trimble (1984)

HERE LIES A HUGE CHUNK of dark gray gneiss, like an enormous body asleep in the streambed. You step onto this dry, barren bedrock in the narrow bottom of Box Canyon. Above, where ocotillos whip their wand-like branches in the hot wind, the desert slopes of loose scree seem lively, active by comparison. By your standards, the quartz- and feldspar-flecked gneiss—formed from Precambrian granite about thirty million years ago—are too old, too heavy to move.

You cast a glance upstream. Suddenly, the canyon bottom no longer

appears so static. It lacks horizontality. There is only the precarious teeter and tilt of boulders, and the acute angle of the slidelike bedrock. There is nothing even-keeled about this landscape. It strikes you that these stones are in suspended animation, ready to roll or change shape with the next rush of wild water.

In short, Box Canyon is an unfinished sculpture. It is in the making, waiting for its carver, water, to return to work. Some blue moon when a drenching downpour does arrive, enough sheer energy and bedload will be carried by flashfloods to cut fluted grooves in the bedrock for hundreds of feet at a stretch. Let loose by erosion beneath them, boulders will roll. As you balance on the lip of a now-dry waterfall, you feel grateful that you are not in the way when a flood rises.

Take a few more steps along the scoured gneiss, and you will come upon another kind of carving. Five bedrock mortars—conical holes tapering down to a half foot or foot in depth—show where women from centuries

past processed mesquite pods. Revolving a stone pestle in a depression in the gneiss, ancient desert dwellers would crush mesquite's sugary pod meal into a flourlike consistency, sorting out the hard seeds within it. Or they would simply rough-mash the pods, add water, let the mixture steep, and later drink this refreshing beverage. Over decades of turning stone upon stone and pods, the mortarholes gradually sank deeper into the bedrock.

It was work, work that consumed considerable time. Looking down at these mesquite mortars, you sense a message from them: "The Old Ones worked where you now play."

The ancient women labored, each toiling perhaps a full day to gather and grind enough mesquite to meet her own caloric needs for five days. They ground out an existence using largely the resources found within a few square miles of the canyon. Yet was it all work? Did the sweetness of drinking mesquite, and the presence of a swimming hole in the shade upstream serve to break the heat, to take the edge off the daily tedium? Was this a place to relax, gossip and recreate as well as to work?

Not far from these five bedrock mortars, the canyon wall cryptically offers an answer. Obscured by the shade which protects them from bleaching, pictographs announce that long ago, art arose from the work done here. The hematite paintings are red lines zig-zagging together across the grain of the canyon wall.

Across the Tucson Basin, on Tumamoc Hill, an O'odham Indian farmer was once shown such zigzags by an archeologist studying petroglyphs scratched into volcanic boulders.

"Those three lines going along together there . . .," the old O'odham man puzzled, ". . . they must be the rainbow. . . . Yes, because look there below them. There are more drawings of people joining hands, doing the round dance, I guess. A rainbow arch is taken around at the start of our rain-bringing dance, and maybe those people who drew this picture did the same thing to bring the rains."

Through such dancing and drawing, the rains were called upon not to move boulders but to bring water and nutrients to the small fields which the Indians tended downstream. In late prehistoric times, even small tributary washes were managed with check dams. Contour terraces adjacent to them were planted. Today, half-buried rocks remind us:

"Here, we made the runoff flow. There, we slowed the waters. And over there, the moisture sank in around the roots of the planted crops."

Wherever you go within Box Canyon's reaches, rocks carry a message. Some might be cobbles chipped out of quarries of a special rock found on Tanque Verde Ridge, microbreccia, by someone making arrowheads a thousand years ago. Others may be quartz

left, banded gneiss

hammerstones or purple rhyolite flakes carried in from other ridges in the Rincons. They tell a simple story:

The Ancient Ones used rocks well, knowing their hardness, their sharpness and the ways in which they fracture. The Hohokam transported special sorts—obsidian, quartz—for miles to help with particular chores.

We now know that some rocks traveled on their own.

Old stones in the Tucson Mountains may have come from the Rincons and Catalinas twenty to thirty miles away on the other side of the valley. Perhaps strata that now underlie Saguaro National Monument West once overlaid the present position of Saguaro National Monument East!

Even if rocks can't tell us the whole story, it's clear that they know their way around.

Call it the mid-Tertiary orogeny, or simply the Great Continental Stretch. Whatever the name, it was a time when southern Arizona began to pull apart. Sedimentary strata similar to those in the Grand Canyon were pulled down as the upper crust was spread thin. The deepening faults put these mudstones, marls, packstones and micrites in touch with recently metamorphosed gneisses. The major faults themselves, gently tilting downward toward the west, became broad zones where rock moving one way was sheared against that moving in another direction. As the Tucson Basin continued to widen with this east-west

stretching and shearing, the limestones above were folded into contorted shapes. The brittle gneiss beneath them fractured where the shear zone reached near the surface. Some of this gneiss became completely exposed for the first time in millions of years.

Whether at or near the surface, this gneiss no longer had the tremendous weight of hundreds of meters of sediment mounted atop it anymore. About twenty million years ago, this "weight loss" changed the shape of the landscape in an amazing way. The gneiss freed of its overlying burdens rose buoyantly, forming the enormous domelike mounds of the Rincons.

The raising of the Rincons was not an isolated mountain-building event. From Mexico's Sonora to Canada's British Columbia, the western portion of the North American continent stretched fifteen to several hundreds of miles during the mid-Tertiary times, twenty to thirty millions of years ago. As it stretched, the earth's crust became deformed. Mountains similar to the Rincons cropped up in numerous places. Yet the Rincons' geological sequence played a pivotal position in helping geologists understand the entire regional pattern. Compared to the better known Basin and Range mountain-building events five to fifteen million million years ago, this recently-uncovered mid-Tertiary orogeny was just as significant in the making of the Western landscape.

petroglyphs; overleaf, Rincon Mountains

The sequence of strata in a mountain range speak discreetly to geologists, allowing them to visualize an order of events that most of us can hardly imagine. Sometimes, however, not even a gifted geoscientist can make order of seeming chaos.

Like that of the Tucson Mountain Chaos.

As you drop westward down the switchbacks from Gates Pass toward Saguaro West, you descend through a fantasy land of crags, crevices, steep cliffs and shallow caves. Look closely at the material which makes up this hodge-podge of shapes. Tucson Mountain Chaos is an amalgam of rhyolitic tuff, a lava and ash mix containing chunks of older rocks as big as Winnebagos, and as anomalous as houseboats stuck in a desert arroyo.

There are lava flows broken off, as if leading from nowhere. Ash spewed out of now-vanished cones which once sat out near Kitt Peak. Rocks liquified with the heat of volcanic blasts, then resolidified in the midst of the fallout of tons of ash. Floating in a Cretaceous tuff, Paleozoic boulders were blown out of a caldera some 200 million years after their formation. This is the Chaos, a geologist's nightmare.

They see shreds of evidence of catastrophic events. The collapse of a crater, the avalanche of older cliffs dropping into red-hot flows eating their way underneath, the inundation of everything by a downpour of airborne ash. All this was followed by differential erosion of hard and soft surfaces which further removed pieces of the already hopeless puzzle. As yet, there is no consensus on how the range of features found here came to be.

An ornery creature, it wildly defies explanation.

A rolling stone gathers no moss. It gathers history.■

sandstone, Tucson Mountains

LAND-BASED SUBSISTENCE IN THE TUCSON BASIN

The grinding stones and contoured terraces found around the Rincons and Tucsons indicate that long ago, people obtained food by working this land—including land now assumed to be "unproductive"—without supplemental irrigation. To the contrary, the Tucson Basin produces over 100 wild plant species and more than twenty animals which native peoples have used as food. In addition, ten cultivated food crops and turkeys were introduced to the Santa Cruz watershed in prehistoric times, further diversifying the dietary options available to desert dwellers. Some of these crops were grown with much less water—often in the form of runoff rather than river diversion irrigation—than the amounts modern farmers apply to their fields today.

Prior to the development of prehistoric farming, native people regularly gathered and hunted foods in the wide range of environmental zones found in the basin. Pinyon nuts, non-bitter acorns, berries and the bases of century plants were among the middle elevation montane foodstuffs that were gathered and stored for leaner times. Saguaro cactus fruit, mesquite pods, cholla cactus buds, wild greens and beans were the mainstays offered from the lower rocky slopes and desert floor. Springs and floodplain streams nurtured plants not found in drier sites. Bands of several families moved between a number of campsites at different times of the year in order to take advantage of the short seasonal pulse of each wild harvest.

As populations grew, the flow of ephemeral and intermittent streams was used to supplement the soil moisture supplies of native weedy plants and introduced domesticates. Corn recently found on Tumamoc Hill is nearly as old as any

found in southern Arizona. Jack beans, amaranths and "wild" barley have a richer history here than in other parts of the U.S. Other obscure crops, such as tepary beans and cushaw squashes, could also be raised with sporadic floodwaters or runoff. The prehistoric Hohokam of southern Arizona selected and fine-tuned a number of vari-

eties of squashes, beans, amaranths and maize to the rigorous environment of the desert. These ancient crops developed greater heat and drought tolerance than most modern-day vegetables.

As Hohokam social organization became increasingly sophisticated, it enabled larger irrigation works to be built and maintained on the Santa Cruz and its major tributaries. Some irrigated crops, such as tobacco and cotton, may have been grown for trade, just as macaws found in the region were probably bred elsewhere and imported here. In later Hohokam phases, agave or century plant cultivation was initiated over thousands of acres of rock-pile gardens on bajadas within sight of the present-day Saguaro National Monument. Meter-high terraces were built for specialty horticultural crops on mountain slopes within just a few miles of Saguaro West. It is apparent that from A.D. 1150 to 1350, the Classic Hohokam had a much more extensive agriculture in a greater variety of environments than can be found in the Tucson Basin today.

This farming base had eroded by the time the first Europeans described the small, riverside rancherias of the O'odham after 1690. Although river-diversion irrigation was still practiced, use of the terraces and rock pile fields had been abandoned. The O'odham, however, did retain a tremendous amount of knowledge regarding wild plants, including uses for most of the 135 local species for which they have names in their native langauge. Throughout their territory in the Sonoran Desert, O'odham plant specialists recognize well over 200 kinds of plants.

Archeologists continue to debate the reasons behind the drastic decline in population and farmed land which occurred in south-central Arizona sometime between A.D. 1350 and 1550. One theory is that the prehistoric human population had grown to the size that it could not maintain food reserves ample enough to tide itself through periods of extreme drought, or through the aftermath of large floods. Although the Tucson Basin can offer a rich and varied supply of food plants, it remains a land of unpredictability.

Pima lima beans in saguaro boot bowl

THE
LIVING NEST:
SAGUARO BOOTS
& SUBTERRANEAN
BURROWS

"The desert is at once a place of sensory deprivation and awesome overload—too little life, too much heat, too little water, too much sky. Its cool shadows offer 'thermal delight,' and yet the desert evokes the terrors of the inferno."

Paul Shepard (1982)

IT'S NOW FAR PAST the point when an old straw sombrero can provide sufficient shelter from the heat. A saguaro nearby, capped with red fruit, looks like a hyperheated thermometer on the verge of spilling its mercury out of the top. Yet it is actually among few that can bear the brunt of July's burning weather. You are among those that must seek refuge. You sight another in your predicament, a bird panting on a branch, anxious to escape the shimmering heat waves. As that bird takes flight, your mind goes with it.

Suddenly you land on the lip of a crusty hole high up on a giant saguaro. Ducking your head inside, you find it uninhabited, inviting. Having left behind the glaring world, you hunker down in the humid shade of the des-

ert's tallest living nest.

A Gila woodpecker carved out this hole over a year ago, flicking chunks of succulent saguaro flesh out of the small opening until a cavity of sufficient size was left for future use. Its lining slowly hardened into a crusty callus almost a half-inch thick, leaving a bottle-shaped "boot" that will persist long after this saguaro's life has expired. You are buffered from the desert heat and dryness by the very succulence of the saguaro itself.

On the southern side of this saguaro, already exposed to the sun's rays for more than four hours, the 10:00 A.M. temperature outside the hole hovers around 104 degrees. In the bottom of the nest-hole itself, the temperature does not surpass ninety degrees. During the daily cycle, the nest seldom heats up above the air temperature outside until after five in the evening, and remains somewhat warmer throughout the night. Overall, it never reaches the hot or cold extremes that a bird or beast would face in the open desert. The boot not only

gilded flicker & nest

maintains a higher humidity, it retains water for months at a time. The pool at the bottom of the boot serves as an evaporative cooler, but also fosters the buzz of mosquitos.

Mosquitos are not enough to discourage refugees from finding comfort here. House finches, starlings and purple martins will dive into saguaro boots during the summer, particularly near the suburban areas. Big brown bats and, infrequently, cactus mice, climb into nest-holes. A dozen kinds of insects, including springtails, swallow bugs, blow flies, wasps, grasshoppers and katydids also gain a foothold on the world within cactus boots.

Certain animal activities advertise the presence of these desert hideaways. They are the jackhammer drummings of the Gila woodpeckers, the *churr, churr* of their territorial calls, and the *flicka-flicka-flicka* of their more cosmopolitan relative, the gilded flicker. These are birds that work hard on new nest-holes in the weeks after the spring fledglings have taken to the air, no longer needing care. These are the noisy but necessary homebuilders which Hispanic-Americans call "carpinteros."

Henry David Thoreau recorded flicker behavior in the eastern temperate forests. His description fits the woodpeckers of the cactus forest as aptly as those in a temperate grove of trees: "So the flicker dashes up through the aisles of the grove, throws up a window here and cackles out of it, and then there, airing the house. It makes its voice ring upstairs and downstairs, and so, as it were, fits it for its habitation and ours, and takes possession."

It may be idle fantasy for a human to imagine turning into a bird, and escaping into a nest-hole. Yet perhaps it is one of humankind's oldest dreams, and the reveries of shady microenvironments are not uncommon among desert dwellers. Gaston Bachelard, the French naturalist, has challenged us to consider this: "If we were to look among the wealth of our vocabulary for verbs that express the dynamics of retreat, we should find images based on animal movements of withdrawal, movements that are engraved in our own muscles. ... A nest, like any other image of rest and quiet, is immediately associated with the image of a simple house ... a wren's nest is a thatched cottage."

For the French, the dream-nest is surely a place of warmth; a harbor from the wind, snow and cold. For the desert dwellers, shelter from the scorching sun, the heat and the dust must come to mind more spontaneously.

Humans are not the only ones who need to be buffered from the sun's blast. Oddly, some of the most successful animals in the desert, from javelina to owls, have no special physical adaptations for tolerating high temperatures. If left out in the open sun on a summer day, these creatures would soon reach their physiological limits.

Instead, little characters such as the elf owls must rely on the saguaro nest-hole for their thermoregulation. These pint-sized predators, found in abundance in Saguaro National Monument, could not produce so many young there during the summer heat were it not for the air-conditioned cubicles provided by the cactus/woodpecker association. Where saguaros are absent in desert areas, elf owls retreat to cooler mountain canyons and nest in oaks and sycamores. The cool microenvironment within saguaro cavities is equivalent to that obtained by climbing another 2,000 feet into the southwestern sierras.

To buffer themselves from the desert's extremes, some animals descend into the earth rather than ascending saguaros or sierras. Even eminently-adapted desert kangaroo rats spend nearly two-thirds of their waking time beneath the ground, even at night when the heat has largely subsided. During the day, the advantages of a subterranean lifestyle are manifest. On a black volcanic rocky slope in the Tucson Mountains, summer surface temperatures may surpass 165 degrees. The soil between rocks gets as hot as 114 for several hours at a time. Yet down in the rodent burrow, temperatures seldom exceed eighty-eight degrees.

The moderate temperatures of rodent burrows are associated with higher relative humidity, just as in the saguaro nest-hole. But in this case, rodent activity has increased the moisture-holding capacity of the soil around the dens, due to the mixing of various-sized soil particles with organic matter from food and feces. This surrounding soil moisture serves as evaporative cooler pads, and the tunnels of the burrow complex channel ventilating air toward the resident rodents. But the favorable soil moisture conditions serve other purposes too, such as aiding in the germination of seeds carried to the burrow.

The living nest of the Bailey's pocket mouse is not within a plant (as for the elf owl), but one in which seeds are planted. Not just seeds of any desert plant, but of a special one: jojoba, the wax-bearing shrub endemic to the Sonoran Desert and the outer coast of lower California.

Within burrow complexes of Bailey's pocket mouse in the Tucson Mountains, as many as thirty-two jojoba seedlings have been found growing clustered together. Ecologist Wade Sherbrooke has observed that particular conditions needed to germinate the

elf owl in saguaro boot

waxy-seeded jojoba—sufficient soil moisture, the absence of light, and a narrow range of warm temperatures—are all met by the pocket mouse burrow. Bailey's pocket mice gather as many as two pounds of jojoba seed for storage in their shallow, subterranean burrows. Although toxic to other rodents, the seeds of this desert shrub are digestible by the Bailey's pocket mice because they have evolved means to detoxify this otherwise nutritious food source. They gradually consume their caches of seeds in the months following the harvest. On occasion, some of the undevoured seeds germinate while in shallow storage. If any of these emerge from the ground and survive past the seedling stage, they eventually benefit the progeny of their seed disperser.

By "sowing" the seeds they carry back from nearby shrubs, and by keeping the soil around their dens moderately disturbed, these pocket mice are inadvertently acting as farmers. Curiously, within the last decade, humankind has begun to propagate jojoba as well, bringing thousands of desert acres into cultivation to obtain the unique products of this shrub with lower water requirements than those of conventional crops. Jojoba's unusual liquid wax has already been incorporated into a variety of shampoos, lotions and heat-stable lubricants now being marketed nationally.

For jojoba seeds to find their way into the homes of Bailey's pocket mice and American consumers, jojoba pollen must first reach "homeward." This pollen must successfully travel from male to nearby female shrubs where flowers, once fertilized, can develop seeds. With the shrubs so sparsely dispersed on desert slopes, and the winds there so wayward, it's a wonder that many miniscule pollen grains ever land on receptive stigmas at all.

And yet, jojoba's own architecture directs the air traffic of pollen grains which come into reach, funneling them towards the female flowers. Each of these flowers is flanked by a pair of upright leaves, which can intersect air flows around the plant. Once intersected, the pollen grains drain down into a "trough" between the leaves. They shower down on the flower hanging below the leaf pair, or onto adjacent flowers further downwind. Female flower shapeliness also "attracts" or deflects pollen, directing more grains toward their target.

A plant lacking these design features has its pollination left up to luck alone. After Karl Nicklas and Steve Buchmann discovered jojoba's architectural assets, they wondered what would happen to its pollen if they removed the leaves or floral bracts which guide this traffic flow. Taking away the pairs of leaves above a series of flowers, they found that less than half as many pollen grains reached their destination on a defoliated branch as on an intact one. Without such architectural guides to pollination, there would be fewer jojoba seed for both mice and men. ▪

CACTUS WREN NESTS AND EVAPORATIVE COOLING

Not everyone can live underground or in the heart of a cactus. Birds that must build their own nests out in the elements will better survive the desert's extremes if the location, orientation and shape of their nests buffer them from these extremes. As ecologists have shown, the proper positioning of a nest in relation to the surrounding environment can make the difference between hatchling success and death.

Cactus wrens build flask-shaped nests of grasses that are then lined with feathers. They are often placed high in the spiney branches of teddy bear cholla and other multi-branched, treelike cacti which offer protection from predators. Oddly, adults and juveniles will sleep in different roosting nests built near one another. Adults do, however, huddle together with hatchlings when they bring food into their nests, and the hatchlings huddle with one another during much of the remaining time. During cooler nights, such huddling can raise the within-nest temperatures as much as forty-three degrees F. since body heat is kept from dissipating by the insulating effects of the nest.

Perhaps a more critical problem comes in summer. Too much heat can accumulate within the nest on hot summer days. Ecologists Robert Ricklefs and Reed Hainsworth discovered that cactus wren nests are often cooler than the ambient temperature in July. They guess that the birds encourage a kind of evaporative cooling within their nests, so that hot winds hitting the nests are cooled down when passing through a moistened "filter." As summer temperatures increase, young wrens tend to defecate more moist feces onto the mat of grass and feathers serving as the nest floor. Three of four nestling wrens excrete as many as 3.7 fluid ounces of water on a hot summer day. Half that amount, when sprinkled on the bottom of the nest cavity, is enough to cool down the nest at least two more degrees.

The ability of moist wren droppings to serve in the cooling of the nests is enhanced by easy movement of air into these nests. If a nest faces into the wind, it allows air to circulate freely into this grass-and-feather flask, dissipating the heat made by the hatchlings and picking up humidity from fecal sacs on the floor. The majority of nests built by cactus wrens in the Saguaro National Monument vicinity have an entrance hole orientation to the southwest, the direction from which the prevailing winds arrive. Verdins also build their little nest enclosures to have southwest-facing openings.

A nest's southwestward orientation actually pays off for its feathered inhabitants. Ornithologist George Austin watched eighty-six nests during the time when eggs hatched and the nestlings fledged. He found that the eggs laid in nests with a southwest orientation had a much higher survivorship of birds than those in nests oriented otherwise. Nests that successfully fledged all their young were more than twice as frequent on the southwest orientation than they were on random orientations. Perhaps a little evaporative cooling goes a long way towards making life more comfortable, even for a desert-loving bird like the cactus wren.

cactus wren

cactus wren nest in cholla

THE RAIN, THE WASH, & THE IMPROBABLE POOL

"Long ago, they say, when the earth was not yet finished, darkness lay upon the water, and they rubbed at each other. The sound they made was like the sound at the edges of a pond. There, on the water, in the darkness, in the noise, and in a very strong wind, a child was born." O'odham legend, translated by Saxton and Saxton (1973)

YOU HAD NOT BEEN HERE since the wintertime, when snowmelt had freshly filled this rock-bottomed pool to the brim, and the overflow dropped off a two-foot-wide waterfall into the gravelly wash ten yards below. Now the snowmelt from the mountains above has ceased to replenish the waterhole. At the lower edge of the shrunken pool, all that remains of the waterfall are twenty-two finger-thick green

ribbons of dried algae, dangling like crumpled crepe paper streamers left after a party. The pond's remaining contents remind you less of water and more of pea soup—you could chew it as easily as you could drink it.

Straining your eyes to see into its depths, you spot darting tadpoles of the canyon treefrog. You catch a glimpse of the erratic glides and dives of aquatic insects, but they are too difficult to identify through the murky broth. You wonder how theses creatures tolerate the range of waterhole conditions that must occur between March and June. The pond undergoes a twenty degree rise in surface temperature, a drastic decrease in oxygen and considerable increases in salinity and turbidity. Tadpoles must be among those which can rapidly adjust to these changing conditions.

Other organisms, unable to acclimate to such extremes, must find other ways to survive. Some amphibians move away to more permanent pools, perhaps where overhanging rocks slow evaporation. Clam shrimps survive only as eggs during drought months, opting for a strategy similar to that of desert wildflowers which lie "asleep" in seed form. In desert ponds, certain crustaceans called copepods slow down metabolism to the point that their maturation is arrested until pool conditions become favorable again. The soupier the waterhole becomes,

above & overleaf, Box Canyon

the more its aquatic inhabitants go dormant. Fewer filter their way through its sludge.

Aquatic species are not the only animals dependent upon the ephemeral pools in Rincon and Tucson mountain canyons. Twenty-five kinds of desert

birds and ten different mammals are known to use such waterholes in the Tucson Basin. Although the remaining brew at this time of year may be too thick to be appetizing to you, bobcat, deer, doves and quail will still stave off thirst and dehydration with this liquid as long as it lasts.

As the perimeter of this pool con-

tracts, and others nearby dry up altogether, wildlife coming for water are placed in closer contact with one another. Competition for the dwindling reserves increases. When a herd of javelina drops down to the pond to drink, a solitary mule deer backs away, stiff-legged, to brush fifty yards away.

The pond is left to the thirsty herd, but not all drink at once. Three or four move up to the water while others feed nearby or simply watch, on alert.

Suddenly, a rattle. The three drinking javelina bolt from the pool. A diamondback rattlesnake slides from the rocks into the mud just above the declining water level. The javelina that had retreated cautiously return to the far side, sharing it with doves that cycle through every few minutes for brief drinks. A jackrabbit approaches near the javelina, but they remain oblivious to it. The snake, meanwhile, continues its warning rattle. Soon, nothing remains but tracks drying in the mud.

When the first summer downpour storms in, it does more than just wash away the old castings of animal tracks. It transforms the pond, the desert surrounding it, everything. An hour ago, after weeks without rain, the drought was broken, and with it went your vision of the Rincons. A rainstorm's sixty-six mile an hour wind sent up enough dust that a fifteen-mile-long mountain range disappeared altogether. Sprigs of creosote bushes were blown prone. Weighty palo verde branches cracked off their trunks and were thrown to the ground. Forty minutes after the downpour, you see lightning still breaking, backlighting the pines on the ridges of the Rincons.

The desert floor has been stained by the rains for the first time in more than two months. You take your shoes off and amble down a desert trail, sidestepping ants, frenzied by the wind and the sporadic light sprinkle that descends again. It is nearing dusk, the cactus wrens are chattering nervously and mourning doves fly wildly in every direction. The winds are still gusty enough to blow a lesser nighthawk yards off course before he recovers. Gambel's quail and desert cottontails bolt out of the bushes. Everyone is running or flying for shelter.

Fortunately, some creatures, such as spadefoot toads, prefer their shelters on the wet side of life. When you arrive back at the waterhole two hours later, after dark has set in, you find spadefoot toads on their first night out of the ground in ten and a half months.

The waterhole you see bears no re-semblance to the one you remember from months before. A shallow, three-foot stream falls over the cliff-face where the algal streamers once hung, and the waterhole remains deepest a few yards back from the rock lip. Side-pools have formed closer to the canyon walls, where the flashfloods hours before scoured out gravel almost down to the bedrock. They dumped new supplies of frothy water and mud. Here, in the sidepools, spadefoots have come to congregate, mate and feed.

They have been drummed out of the ground by the sound of thunder and tumbling raindrops, after working themselves closer to the surface during this last month. The energy gained from insects swallowed down last year

is largely depleted. They have tolerated a tremendous internal build-up of urea to slow down their moisture loss to the surrounding dried-out soil. Now released, they instantly feed on newly-hatched insects released by the rains, and soak themselves in the freshly-filled pools.

Just as immediate as their desire to

Western diamondback rattlesnake

47

eat is their urge to mate. The males begin a lamblike bleating, and search for mates. A male finds a receptive female, then latches onto her with his specialized nuptial pads. After coupling, the female spews out ribbonlike masses of thousands of eggs. After just a few hours following the storm, the spadefoots have completed their mating for the entire year.

In Avra Valley, thirty-five miles away from Saguaro West, naturalist Clay May and Dennis Cornejo documented the fastest life-cycle of any amphibian in the West. Under ideal conditions of growth in hot, detritus-filled waters, Couch's spadefoot can metamorphose into toadlets in nine days after being dropped as an egg. Without this rapid life-cycle, the entire population's progeny could be wasted if another flood or if a severe drought came before metamorphosis is completed. And should their eggs take more than three days to hatch, so that competitors have time to consume the pond's food supplies, the subsequent tadpoles and toadlets will not gain enough energy to develop.

In Avra Valley and the Tucson Basin, the first flashfloods flow thick with nitrogen-rich organic matter. In a landscape dominated by tree legumes such as palo verde, ironwood and mesquite, tremendous amounts of nitrogenous litter are produced over the year. With much of it falling to the ground after hard frosts or during droughts, this litter lies beneath the trees' canopies until a storm arises forceful enough to float it away.

As rivulets on the slopes braid together and drain to canyon watercourses, the phosphates and nitrates carried by this runoff froth up into a beerlike head. If the force of the floods is broken or slowed, the waters drop this suspended bedload, and much of the desert-derived nutrients are deposited. This deposition can take place at a bedrock barrier, at the bottom of a canyon, or if the flood is charged enough, the nutrients may reach permanent stream sections of the Gila and Colorado rivers.

The floodplain vegetation along these watercourses is particularly lush, thanks to this natural fertilization and irrigation. Early Tucson Basin farmers took advantage of the nutrient-rich soils that were regularly replenished on these floodplains, and until recently the most productive crops in Pima County were nursed by this fertility. Today, most fields within the Santa Cruz watershed are protected from floods, and receive their

alum root

irrigation from pumped groundwater.

Even those southern Arizona farmers who use groundwater owe some thanks to the Rincon Mountain watershed for recharging the aquifers that they draw upon. Thanks to the far-sighted founding fathers of Saguaro National Monument, most of the Rincon range was conserved, not just the cactus forest itself. Without timber-cutting in its forest, or open pit mining and heavy grazing on its flanks, there remains enough natural ground cover to slow the flow of runoff draining into the basin below. The floods are less "flashy," with lower peak flows from a forested or grass-covered watershed than from a barren one. The relatively natural state of the Rincon Mountains therefore buffers and protects the city of Tucson from more damaging floods.

More than 200 miles away from the Rincons, on the delta of the Colorado River, Cocopah Indian and Mexican fishermen bring in a catch that is not-so-remotely dependent upon desert watersheds as one might suspect. Although the fish themselves do not come from the Rincons, part of their nourishment does. Nitrogen concentrations in Sonoran Desert runoff and floodwaters are three to four times higher than those from other watersheds in the Western U.S. The flash-floods roaring down desert mountain arroyos carry enough dissolved nitrogen to larger, perenially-flowing rivers to provide the basis for their algae production. Algae then become the food

upon which many fish and other aquatic life depend. As hydrologists studying flashfloods have concluded, "Permanent desert streams . . . owe much of their chemical and biological nature to fleeting cloudburst storms which may have occurred miles and months away on rocky desert landscapes."

Life within the Sonoran Desert—from the thorn-covered plant to the Colorado River toad—is recharged by these fleeting moments. Desert ecology is the integral story of the rain, the wash and improbable pools. ■

storm over Rincon Peak

50

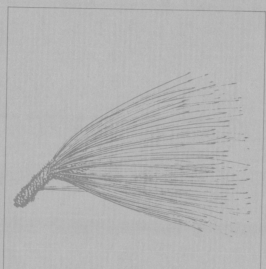

THE ISLAND IN THE CLOUDS: THE RINCON UPLANDS

"I remember—I must have been five or six years old—my father would put me on a big horse and we would go for a ride and he would say to me: Look mi hijito *[my little son], do you see that little animal over there? That animal's name is such and such. He lives in this way. You will see him in such and such a condition and these are the places you will find him. . . .*

"He had home-steaded up in the Rin-con Mountains, above Colossal Cave. . . . It was an isolated place, but my father liked it. My grandfather told him that it was like [what] he used to see in Spain. The mountains, the trees, everything reminded him of Spain." Leonardo Martinez, Tucson native, in Martin and Bernal, 1983

SEVEN HOURS OF HIKING ever-upward have just earned you a 360-degree view of a mass of rugged ter-rain—terrain so mind-boggling, the vision humbles you.

As the wind roars against your ears, your eyes roam a land to the east and northeast once known as the *Gran Apachería*, where the Chiricahua and other Apache bands once circulated. Southward, your vision reaches to Sonora, Mexico. To the west, you scan the desert country of the O'odham which circumscribes their sacred mountain, Baboquivari. To the north-west, the formidable ridges of the Santa Catalinas block a more distant vista. Fifteen mountain ranges can be seen, rising out of a sea of desert and short-grass prairie. Some are shrouded in cumulus, obscur-ing them from full view.

You have gone as far as you can go, to the top of a largely barren, hummocky chunk of rock loom-ing large at 8,482 feet above sea level. Dive-bombing white-throated swifts, daredevil stunt pi-lots in tuxedos, zip past you. They zoom off, chasing another bird of their own feather. Two swifts of opposite sexes catch the same up-draft, mate in mid-air, then freefall together over the cliffs until buoyed by another updraft. While watching them tumble, you instinc-tively grip the rocks around you, as if to secure a firmer place for yourself here at the limits of the earth.

Where you sit, holding the ground, catching your breath, ladybugs abound. They swarm over you, for you

Rincon highlands

are just as good a shelter as any wind-pruned, bonsai-style shrub nearby . Canyon live oak, mock-orange, buck-brush, netleaf oak and pinyon pine—here is the same set of woodland plants found in nearly every range from the Colorado Plateau's Mogollon Rim to the Sierra Madre Occidental of northern Mexico. In more sheltered, northwest-facing troughs on the side of Rincon Peak, you see madroñe, New Mexico locusts, Douglas-fir, aspen, cinquefoil, choke-cherries and three more kinds of pines. Having seen most of these same characters on Mount Lemmon, or in the Sierra Ancha in central Arizona, or down in the Chiricahuas, you're surprised how familiar rather than how foreign the peak's plants are to you. You have landed on another island in an archipelago in which each isle is a minor variant of the others, but all are within the same current.

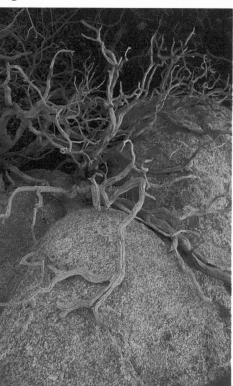

This current is what plant geographer Steve McLaughlin calls the Apachian floristic element—a cluster of plants most frequently found together in the mountain ranges of southeastern Arizona, southwestern New Mexico, and the adjacent corners of Sonora and Chiricahua. It shares some plants with the Rocky Mountains of the U.S. and Canada (like coral-root and alum-root) and others with the Sierra Madres of Mexico (like lady's tresses), but pledges allegiance to neither of these larger cordilleras. This is because it safekeeps a fair number of additional plants that are found *only* within this smaller region. They characterize a peculiarly southwestern plant assemblage strewn along the lowest, driest section in the backbone of the entire North American continent. The Apachian flora might just as well be called the "small of the back" plants.

The best known Apachian indicators are upland cacti and succulents, but they also include dwellers at the desert edge: the thousand-leaved acacia and the Rincon Mountain feathertree, which is the mascot of the Arizona Native Plant Society. Several wild beans and tick-clovers, a catsclaw, various giant-hyssops or horsemints, a thoroughwort, a green-flowered pincushion, a purple hedgehog, Bartram's succulent echeveria and a tall, yellow-blooming mescal are among the plants found in middle elevations of the Rincons that are endemic or restricted to the Apachian region. Some of these reach clear up to 7,000 or 8,000 feet.

Above these elevations, you sense the shadows of Rocky Mountain or Sierra Madrean forests. Yet the fabrics of these influences are frayed here, for the Rincons are a distant outlier from both. Apache pine, a Sierra Madrean dominant, reaches the Santa Ritas just to the south, but not this far. No alpine fir can be found in the Rincons today, although it is as close as the Santa Catalinas and the Pinaleños. Rocky Mountain birds such as the golden-crowned kinglet and orange-crowned warbler seldom range into the Rincons, yet they are resident in the Catalinas and northward. Other birds such as mountain chickadees, warbling vireos and yellow-rumped warblers commonly breed in the Rincons and Catalinas, but rarely nest in the Santa Ritas or Huachucas to the south. The mountain ranges around the Rincons have long marked a tension zone between the life of the Rockies and that of the Sierra Madre.

This tension zone may have moved up or down, and northward or southward, depending upon the prevailing weather of a particular historical period. About 14,000 years ago, Arizona cypress and Douglas-fir could be found in the nearby Catalinas as low as 5,100 feet, near where the upper limit of desert now occurs. During the Pleistocene, coniferous woodlands dipped into the Tucson Basin thousands of feet lower than they are found today. Then storm patterns shifted from mild, wet winters and cool, dry summers to something more like the biseasonal rainfall pattern found in the Sonoran Desert today. With greater summer rainfall, plants and animals with more southerly affinities may have expanded upward into the Rincons. The ranges of northern species may have contracted at the same time, but such species still make up a larger portion of the Rincon's higher elevation flora.

The tides of northerly and southerly influences may rise or ebb against its flanks, but the Rincons remain "high country." Eighty square miles of Rincon woodland and coniferous forest, much of it in Saguaro National Monument, serve as a highland haven for hundreds of lifeforms that could not survive in the deserts below. About seventy to eighty bird species, fifteen to twenty mammals and 600-700 plants can be found in the Rincons that are absent from the Tucson Mountains. Orographic precipitation—the rain made by clouds marching upslope—has always kept the Rincons wetter than the surrounding basins. Whereas the cactus forest at 3,100 feet receives twelve to fifteen inches of rain a year, Manning Camp in Saguaro East at 8,000 feet is drenched with double those quantities, if rainfall and snowfall both are taken into account.

Remarkable feats can be accomplished in this upland haven—feats that no one but a magician could pull off in the desert below. Around the turn of the century, a Dutchman dry-farmed potatoes near Spud Rock Cabin, at 7,200 feet. An orchard of apples, peaches and pears persisted for years at Manning Camp, surviving largely on rainfall. The relief from desert heat offered at this site was sufficient for Levi Howell Manning, Surveyor General of the Arizona Territory, to have had a wagon trail built up to his cabins there, facilitating his escape from the lowlands for the summer. In 1906, the Mannings hauled a piano up the trail, and for a while, the music of civilization joined that of the winds and the wildlife.

If that old wagon trail still ran from Manning Camp to Tucson below, and you were to walk it downward 5,000 feet to the desert floor, you could literally *hear* the changes in environments along the way. Better yet, you could start the descent from the Mica Mountain lookout, or from Rincon Peak, and trail down from these summits through a range of sounds. The shifts in mixes of bird songs along the way signal changes in microclimate, plant architecture and food availability.

Begin your descent from the mixed conifer forest at around 8,400 to 8,000 feet. There, on a northwest face, you can hear the roar of the wind in the firs above. From the deep shade of the forest floor, you can hear the clear, ethereal flutework of the hermit thrush—a single, long initiating note, a pause, followed by clusters of ascending or descending notes, each cluster in a different pitch. Breeding in the boreal shade, nesting in a cup of moss and grass, the hermit thrush is among Arizona's finest crooners. Its songs, its soft *chuck*-like call, are characteristic of the Rincon firs, as are the hairy woodpecker's *chink* and rattle, and the western flycatcher's strident *whee-seet*. Although not restricted to this forest type, the hoots of spotted owls, the scolding *shook-shook-shook* of Stellar's jays, and the *seet-seet-seet-seet-seet-TRRRRs* of yellow-rumped warblers are frequently heard in the Douglas and white firs. These are the rough-hewn languages of rugged mountaineers, the cold-hardy breeding birds of the montane coniferous forest.

Although they range into the mixed conifers, other sounds are more typical of the widespread pine forest found between 8,000 and 8,600 feet. Ponderosa and white pine dominate the cover, with Gambel's oaks, New Mexican locusts and snowberries in the openings. There, the *gobble* of wild turkeys turns into *keow-keow* as they leave the ground at dusk for roosts in the tall pines. Amidst the *chick-a-zee-zee-zees* of a dozen mountain chickadees, your ears pick out the singular rising and falling whistle of a solitary vireo. The piping of pygmy nuthatches, the warbling whistle of Mexican bluebirds and the chucking hepatic tanagers arise from nearby pine snags, amidst buckbrush and bracken ferns. The call of another pine zone breeder reminds you of the region's Hispanic heritage—you could swear that Coues' peewee was calling *Jose-Maria*!

The next zone continues the cacophony of acorn and pine-nut eaters and trunk-walking insect gleaners, but the pine-oak forest at 5,300 to 8,000 feet is more open, more exposed. The unforgettable *whack-up!, whack-up!, whack-up!* reverberates through the woodland, as an acorn woodpecker protects his family's

acorn cache from potential robbers. These highly social clowns will also call out *Jacob!* to one another, and they nest communally in hollow limbs of oaks and pines. Though sexually promiscuous within the roosting group, they have great fidelity to their storage tree, which may keep enough acorns to last them through several bad years.

Yet their social flare cannot compare with that of the Mexican jays, which communally feed the young of the flock as well as nesting females unwilling to leave eggs just before their hatching. Over half a young jay's food may come from family "helpers" rather than the parents themselves. The flock as a whole is highly coordinated, making conversational *clucks* and *quicks* to keep one another aware of their whereabouts. If one becomes threatened by a bobcat, rattlesnake or skunk, the alarmed jay cries out a high-pitched *WHEET! WHEET!* and the entire flock mobs the adversary until it flees.

Even more than the buckbrush and Oregon grapes of the pine-oak forest, the chaparral woodland extending down to 4,400 feet offers birds such as scrub jays a variety of berries. The small fruits of manzanitas, silk tassel and Arizona rosewood, plus the lemon-berries of the fire-resistant squaw-bushes provide additional nutrition to these birds. Bushtits and bridled titmice extend through these woodlands

spotted owl

and along streams trailing off into the desert, acrobatically foraging on these berries and the insects found around them. As they roam in little bands, you hear their noisy fussing: *tsit, lisp, clenk, tee-wit, tsick-cheeee.* Insectivorous blue-gray gnatcatchers sometimes add their wheezy *zpee*s and *cheee*s to all these scraping and scratching sounds.

Eleven kinds of woodland birds go no farther down the mountainside than the lowest oak at a little over 4,000 feet. Yet somewhere near that final streamside oak, the ocotillo, saguaro and mesquite are attracting an entirely different crowd of songsters. Whereas higher-elevation paintbrushes and penstemons attract broad-tailed, blue-throated and Rivoli's hummingbirds, the ocotillos and wildflowers below more frequently feed Anna's, Costa's and the broad-billed. The forests harbor red-shafted flickers while saguaros house gilded flickers and Gila woodpeckers. The Rincon aspens shelter brown-throated wrens, and the desert scrub would seem quiet without the noisy *churr*-ing

of the cactus wren. Down below, ash-throated flycatchers continue where the Western flycatchers leave off.

So-called "desert" birds, such as gnatcatchers, crissal thrashers and brown towhees actually begin their music above the saguaro forest, in the mesquite-shindagger-gramagrass zone sometimes called the "semidesert grassland." The poorwill will call his own name from these foothill vantage points, and Scott's orioles love to do their melodic piping from the tall stalks of yuccas, agaves and desert spoons. In the Rincons, this is a steep landscape, with the hotter, drier desert not too far ahead of you. With the exception of the saguaros, all other plants have shrunk as you have moved from forest toward desert. They will continue to shrink, and go underground—investing less in water-transpiring above ground growth and more in water-storing roots and tubers—as you descend to the creosote flats on the valley floor.

The tension zone between the grassy savanna and cactus-dominated

sparrow nest in prickly pear

desert occurs in the Rincons between 3,500 and 4,300 feet. This battle line has moved downslope since cattle were eliminated from the monument, indicating that overgrazing had diminished grasses and ushered in thorny desert shrubs. But once you drop below this line, you can hardly go a hundred yards without hearing a white-winged dove's *Who-cooks-for-you!* from a saguaro top or a curve-billed thrasher's liquid *Whit-wheat!* from the canopy of a palo verde. There is enough open ground here for roadrunners to catch their prey. The elf owl's puppylike yips and rasps and the high-pitched *flicka* of its saguaro nest-hole maker dominate the cactus forest's sounds at different times of the day.

As you move off the rocky, cactus-covered upper bajada, saguaros decrease while cholla, creosote, bursage and brittlebush make up a larger percentage of the sparse cover. Cactus wrens, Gambel's quail and black-tailed gnatcatchers find nesting and roosting sites in this simpler cover. Those that need tall song posts, observation posts and tree or cactus cavities for nesting are left behind. In the most monotonous desert areas—the silty flats of pure creosotebush—only the *cheet-cheet-chee* of black-throated sparrows and the hollow *cooo* of mourning doves can still be heard.

You have trailed down from stone-faced mountain summits to the edge of a desert city. As it has converted creosote to lush Mediterranean landscaping, complete with palms, oleanders and olives, Tucson has attracted a different set of birds. Where flats were built upon, and where imported verdure was bolstered with groundwater irrigation, gnatcatchers and desert sparrows said *Adios.* Black-chinned hummingbirds, mockingbirds and cardinals mistook these instant green belts for the riparian woodlands which edge larger washes. Inca doves moved up from Mexico in the 1870s, and have spread through the cities of the Southwest via the irrigation canals and farms which connect them. The house sparrow—a European

curved-bill thrasher

immigrant—arrived in Tucson in 1903, and found ways to lodge its nests in the crevices and crannies of adobe ranch houses and Mission-style city homes.

Perhaps the most telling indicator of Tucson's biological transition this century is another European immigrant—the highly-adaptable starling. Starlings were first seen in Arizona just after World War II, and arrived at the University of Arizona campus in 1949. They spread all over downtown Tucson, then out into the suburbs, and they can now be found colonizing saguaro nest-holes on the skirts of the Tucson Mountains. Ornithologist Allan Phillips has grumbled, "Their recent increase in Arizona bodes ill for our native woodpeckers and other hole-nesters such as the purple martin, small owls and . . . flycatchers. . . . Perhaps they will not extend far out into the saguaros, but at any rate it is disgusting to see the martins arriving in May to inspect saguaro holes already full of the abominable starling families—sometimes two families in a single saguaro!"

Gregarious, aggressive and audacious in their behavior, starlings will perhaps be thought of one day as part of the local color in the Tucson Basin. They have quickly learned to imitate the songs of native desert birds, and can even pull off a cowboy-style *Whoo-eee!* now and then. ■

GLOBE-BERRY,
JAVELINA
&
MAN

"... generations to come will be frustrated unless they are safeguarded with national reserve systems ... where parcels of land are chosen to achieve a maximum protection of organic diversity. Otherwise hundreds of species will continue to vanish each year without so much as the standard double Linnaean names to record their existence. Each takes with it millions of bits of genetic information, a history ages long, and potential benefits to humanity left forever unmeasured.... Every species allowed to go extinct, is a slide down the ratchet, an irreversible loss for all."

Edward O. Wilson (1984)

THEY WILL TELL YOU THAT the chance of seeing it is slim. It is a kind of plant so rare that you'd be lucky to ever stumble across even a small patch of it. What's more, it's cryptic, hard to spot. You can go places where the Tumamoc globe-berry has been found in years past, without encountering a single plant. Why? If it is the wrong season, or a drought year altogether, the plant will be underground, out of action and out of sight. It will be dormant, waiting for more soil moisture before it makes its next appearance. It is the seldom-seen star of Saguaro West, the reclusive gourd of the Tucson Mountains, and it is found nowhere outside of the Sonoran Desert.

Yet some summer day when you are *not* looking for it, you will meet *Tumamoca macdougalii* in a spot where you least expect it. You will be within a short distance of the Tucson Mountains, but surrounded by rock and soil quite different from the volcanic slopes where this plant was first discovered on nearby Tumamoc Hill about the turn of the century. Hanging from a waist-high branch of a palo verde tree, a fleshy red berry the size of a shooter marble will catch your eye. You will trace its stringy vine down to a constellation of star-shaped but inconspicuous, moth-pollinated flowers that are nearly the same color as the palo verde branches upon which they are trellised. The small, tri-lobed leaves are just as easy to overlook, lost in the canopy of the palo verde, and among its understory of herbs and grasses.

Without the fruit having ripened to a

tumamoc globe-berry

reddish blush, you would have a tough time distinguishing the presence of this rare plant from its background of similarly-hued desert shrubbery. Yet for a few weeks each summer, they are draped around their nurse plants like bright ornamental lights strung on

The sprawling shoots of *Tumamoca* stem from a thickened woody crown which caps several succulent, tapering tubers. These underground water storage organs are what tide *Tumamoca* over during the dry times of the year. They are the form in which the plant

perseveres for most of the year, resurrecting itself to life above ground from late June to late September. If a drought hits as early as August, the leaves may begin to drop immediately. The spindly stems will shrink in thickness, break in strong winds, then crumble. Come back in November, and you will be hard-pressed to find a sign of vines that had reached out several feet the summer before. Sometimes a new seedling can be

electric cords around a Christmas tree. They don't last long before the violent late summer storms knock them down, leaving them to ants which team up to roll them back towards their colony's hill. Or perhaps fruit-eating birds disperse the seeds, gaining carotene to maintain their plumage color by ingesting the vitamin-rich pulp.

found nearby that has germinated in the mother plant's shadow. Otherwise, there are no persistent fruits hanging around, as with other desert gourds. The Tumamoc globe-berry produces hardly any litter. It barely burdens the earth with its presence.

Ecologists Frank Reichenbacher, Linda Leigh and Clay May are among the fortunate few who have stumbled upon more than one patch of *Tumamoca*. At several of the sites where they have encountered it, something in addition to the plants themselves made them pause: holes in the ground; saucer-shaped excavations in the earth not far from extant globe-berry plants.

From stems, leaves and rootlets remaining in the holes, from nearby animal tracks left in the dust, and from talking with zoologists who knew the patterns of digging and feeding of various desert mammals, Frank confirmed that javelina had probably eaten *Tumamoca* which until recently had persisted where the holes now stand. Javelinas are not alone among the wild piglike peccaries in their predilection for tubers, especially those of cucurbits. *Tumamoca*, like the more common perennial-rooted desert gourds, are in the squash family, and have a distinctive odor—like milk regurgitated by an infant—which javelina can apparently tune in on. Traveling in small, female-dominated herds, javelinas communicate to each other with vocal, scent and body language when one of them has found underground food in an area where it is safe to eat. Perhaps the sour milk smell of the plant, when released by the chewing of one collared peccary, gives the others in the javelina herd a cue that aids their search for other plants. They seek out the same scent nearby, then begin rooting with their tapered snouts, chewing, biting and using their

feet to help unearth the tubers.

In places where it would take hours for you and me to find by sight even a few plants of *Tumamoca*, a javelina herd can efficiently seek them out by smell. At one such site, they consumed more than half the adult plants

within a single growing season, significantly reducing reproduction in the population. Reichenbacher estimates that javelina foraging can cause as much as eighty percent mortality of adult plants over just one season.

However, Frank Reichenbacher and others do not fear that javelinas are possibly *causing* a rare Sonoran Desert

globe-berry vine in palo verde

saguaro forest, Tucson Mountains

plant to go extinct. Wild peccary herd movements are such that they may only rarely feed in a particular place where *Tumamoca* grows, and do not damage other stands of this plant at all.

What disturbs Frank is that any loss of these plants must now be of concern, because land use is rapidly changing over the limited area where this desert endemic species grows. While javelina herds may temporarily reduce the reproduction of a patch of *Tumamoca*, human destruction of its habitat is more pervasive. With increasing pressure by man evident in most of its range, it's no wonder that the naturally rare *Tumamoca macdougalii* is now recommended for endangered species status by the U.S. government.

A century of overgrazing and firewood cutting greatly reduced the protection afforded to globe-berry vines by their nurse plants. Some biologists speculate that these factors may have also caused the local extirpation of birds that formerly must have been major seed dispersers for this plant. More recently, the growth of Tucson and its Avra Valley bedroom commuity satellites have encroached upon a prime habitat of *Tumamoca*. There is little doubt that thousands of plants have been uprooted or buried during the last two decades of home-building and doublewide-trailer parking. Today, pipelines and canals are proposed in areas where some of the 1982 known plants of Tumamoc globe-berry grow in the U.S., and some plants will have

to be rescued before building begins. Yet even if you were to be able to count every plant of this species that remains in existence, it is unlikely that this number exceeds 10,000. Reichenbacher believes it may be closer to 5,000. Less than twenty percent of the known plants are reproductive and large enough to withstand droughts of any length. Many of the remaining plants will be swallowed up during the next decade as Tucson growth continues.

Fortunately, there is one place where the Tumamoc globe-berry is officially protected, where the bulldozers cannot reach. During a four-day, on-foot search of several square miles of Saguaro National Monument's Tucson Mountain Unit, biologists encountered only fifteen plants—averaging one plant found per 150 acres explored. The plants represent less than one percent of all the known Tumamoc globe-berries, but may be the most critical to this species' long-term survival.

As Tucson's population grows, remaining patches of *Tumamoca* become more and more like islands sticking out above the rising tide of urbanization. The environment surrounding these islands is less and less like them—even if not paved over and built upon, it is degraded by dirt bikes, dumping, and introduction of exotic, competitive weeds. If the island patches of *Tumamoca* are too small for its pollinators and seed dispersers to have all their ecological needs met, the chances are high that neither they

overleaf, Tucson Basin

nor the globe-berry populations can persist there indefinitely. If a javelina herd that once roamed a wide range is now forced to feed in a much smaller area, it is more likely that *Tumamoca* present in that smaller area will be affected adversely.

Thus Saguaro National Monument constitutes this desert plant's best ground for persistence, even though the monument's boundaries were not set up with the knowledge that *Tumamoca* would fall within them. Because Saguaro West is large enough for javelina to move and feed freely on a variety of plant resources, it is unlikely that they will be constrained to one area where *Tumamoca* will become their exclusive target. What's more, the globe-berry may someday be dispersed and establish itself in other protected areas adjacent to existing stands within the Monument. In smaller patches stranded within urban areas, adjacent habitat suitable for colonization may no longer exist.

Still, there is no denying the fact that the Saguaro National Monument units are themselves becoming islands in an ocean of man-made environments that differ vastly in diversity, scale and capacity for long-term habitability. The twenty-four-square-mile Saguaro West may have ample habitat for *Tumamoca* and its animal associates, but can it indefinitely support wide-ranging carnivores? What happens to the large vertebrates that venture out of its boundaries, and onto the roads and lots of the surrounding neighborhoods? What happened to the bighorn sheep, known to be in the Rincons just a few decades ago? Can the Saguaro East's ninety-nine square miles sustain separate gene pools of black bear, ringtail cat and cougar, or must there be some gene flow with animals in the Santa Catalina, Santa Rita, Pinaleño and Dragoon mountains to keep these populations healthy? If urban growth between these mountain ranges cuts off sporadic migration from one to the next, what are the evolutionary consequences?

Biologists are attempting to answer such questions today, for they fear that we may diminish the great value of a national park or monument in preserving natural diversity if we degrade everything around it. We cannot be complacent that we "have saved enough" if we set aside some acreage within the National Park System, but do not manage adjacent lands as if they too mattered.

The ultimate answers to such questions may have as much to do with conserving what we can't see as they do with what we can see. Nature poet Wendell Berry has urged us to care for "the unseeable animal," the one that nobody has ever seen, even if it means that we never see it. And perhaps for the sake of an unidentified nocturnal moth, for the sake of a scent-stimulated javelina herd, and for our own sake, we should extend our care to a plant that spends most of its time underground. ■

FURTHER READING

GENERAL

Alcock, John. 1985. *Sonoran Desert Spring*. University of Chicago Press, Chicago, IL.

Davis, Goode P., Jr. 1982. *Man and Wildlife in Arizona: The American Exploration Period, 1824-1865*, Neil B. Carmony and David E. Brown (ed.s). Arizona Game and Fish Department, Phoenix, AZ.

Gilbreath, Robert I. 1985. *Miniature Flowers: A Desert Search*. Northland Press, Flagstaff, AZ.

Krutch, Joseph Wood. 1983. *The Desert Year*. University of Arizona Press, Tucson, AZ.

MacMahon, James. 1985. *Deserts*. Random House/Audubon Society Nature Guides, New York, NY.

McGinnies, William G. 1982. *Discovering the Desert*. University of Arizona Press, Tucson, AZ.

Nabhan, Gary Paul and Mirocha, Paul. 1985. *Gathering the Desert*. University of Arizona Press, Tucson, AZ.

Olin, George. 1977. *House In The Sun*. Southwest Parks and Monuments Association, Tucson, AZ.

Robinson, Mary and Priehs, T.J. (ed.s). 1984. *Cactus Forest Drive*. Southwest Parks and Monuments Association, Tucson, AZ.

Shelton, Napier and Dodge, Natt. 1972. *Saguaro National Monument, Arizona*. U.S. Government Printing Office, Washington, D C.

Steenbergh, Warren F. and Lowe, Charles H. 1977-1983. *Ecology of the Saguaro*. Volumes 1-3. U.S. Department of Interior National Park Service, Washington, DC.

CHAPTER REFERENCES (In order of first citation)

The Long-Lived Giant and the Ephemeral Bellyflower

Bigelow, J., Jr. 1958. *On the Bloody Trail of Geronimo*. Westernlore Press, Los Angeles, CA.

Barcikowski, Wayne and Nobel, Park S. 1984. Water relations of cacti during dessication: distribution of water in tissues. *Botanical Gazette* 145: 110-115.

Schmidt-Nielson, K. 1954. *Desert Animals*. Oxford University Press, London, England.

Steenbergh, Warren F. and Lowe, Charles H. 1983. *Ecology of the Saguaro III: Growth and Demography*. National Park Service, Washington, DC.

Nobel, Park S. 1980. Morphology, nurse plants, and minimum apical temperatures for young *Carnegiea gigantea*. *Botanical Gazette* 141: 188-191.

McAuliffe, Joseph R. 1984. Sahuaro-nurse tree associations in the Sonoran Desert: competitive effects of sahuaros. *Oecologia* 64: 319-321.

Mulroy, Thomas and Rundel, Philip W. 1977. Annual plants: adaptations to desert environments. *BioScience* 27: 109-114.

Inouye, Richard S. 1980. Density-dependent germination response by seeds of desert annuals. *Oecologia* 46: 235-238.

Martin, William E.; Ingram, Helen; Laney, Nancy K.; and Griffin, Adrian H. 1984. *Saving Water in a Desert City*. Resources for the Future, Washington, DC.

The Saguaro Freeze/Bacteria Controversy

Nobel, Park S. 1980. Morphology, surface temperatures, and northern limits of columnar cacti in the Sonoran Desert. *Ecology* 61: 1-7.

Anonymous. No date. History of Saguaro National Monument. Manuscript on file, Saguaro National Monument East, Tucson, AZ.

Lowe, Charles H. and Steenbergh, Warren F. 1981. On the Cenozoic ecology and evolution of the Sahuaro *(Carnegiea gigantea)*. *Desert Plants* 3: 83-87.

Gill, L.S. 1942. Death in the desert. *Natural History* 50: 22-26.

Howes, P.G. 1954. *The Giant Cactus Forest and Its World.* Duell, Sloan and Pearce, New York, NY.

Alcorn, S.M. and May, C. 1962. Attrition of a saguaro forest. *Plant Disease Reporter* 43: 156-163.

Steenbergh, Warren F. and Lowe, Charles H. 1977. *Ecology of the Saguaro II: Reproduction, Germination, Establishment, Growth, and Survival of the Young Plant.* National Park Service, Washington, DC.

Barker, B.C.M. and Starmer, W.T. (ed.s). 1982. *Ecological Genetics and Evolution: The Cactus-Yeast-Drosophila Model System.* Academic Press, Sydney.

Bedrock Mortars, Contoured Terraces, and the Underlying Chaos

Trimble, Stephen. 1984. *Long's Peak: A Rocky Mountain Chronicle.* Rocky Mountain Natural History Association, Estes Park, CO.

Simpson, Kay and Wells, Susan J. 1984. *Archeological Survey in the Eastern Tucson Basin.* Volume III. Western Archeological and Conservation Center, Tucson, AZ.

Krantz, Robert. 1985. *The Geologic History of the Rincon Mountains, Including Saguaro National Monument.* Saguaro National Monument Archives, Tucson, AZ.

Davis, G.H. and others. 1974. Recumbent folds—focus of an investigative workshop in tectonics. *Journal of Geological Education* 204-208.

Chronic, Halka. 1983. *Roadside Geology of Arizona.* Mountain Press, Missoula, MT.

Land-Based Subsistence in the Tucson Basin

Fish, Suzanne K. and Fish, Paul R. (ed.s). 1984. *Prehistoric Agricultural Strategies in the Tucson Basin.* Arizona State University Department of Anthropology, Tempe, AZ.

Hodgson, Wendy Caye. 1982. *Edible Native and Naturalized Plants of the Sonoran Desert North of Mexico.* Arizona State University Master's Thesis, Tempe, AZ.

Nabhan, Gary Paul. 1985. Native crops of Aridoamerica: conservation of regional gene pools. *Economic Botany*, 39(4): 387-399.

Fish, S.K.; Fish, P.R.; Miksicek, C.; and Madsen, J. 1985. Prehistoric agave cultivation in southern Arizona. *Desert Plants* 7: 107-113.

Nabhan, Gary Paul. 1983. *Papago Fields: Arid Lands Ethnobotany and Agricultural Ecology.* University of Arizona Ph.D Dissertation, Tucson, AZ.

The Living Nest: Saguaro Boots and Subterranean Burrows

Shepard, Paul. 1982. *Nature and Madness.* Sierra Club Books, San Francisco, CA.

Krizman, R.D. 1964. *The Saguaro Tree-Hole Microenvironment in Southern Arizona I: Winter.* University of Arizona Master's Thesis, Tucson, AZ.

Soule, O.H. 1964. *The Saguaro Tree-Hole Microenvironment in Southern Arizona II: Summer.* University of Arizona Master's Thesis, Tucson, AZ.

Bergman, Charles. 1984. Face-to-face with the stalwart imp of cactus country. *Smithsonian:* 122-125.

Bachelard, Gaston. 1964. *The Poetics of Space.* Beacon Press, Boston, MA.

Shroeder, Gene R. 1979. Foraging behavior and home range utilization of the bannertail kangaroo rat *(Dipodomys spectabilis).* *Ecology* 60: 657-665.

Prakash, I., and Ghosh, P.K. 1975. *Rodents in Desert Environments.* W. Junk, The Hague.

Sherbrooke, Wade C. 1976. Differential acceptance of toxic jojoba seed *(Simmondsia chinensis)* by four Sonoran Desert heteromyid rodents. *Ecology* 57: 596-602.

Niklas, Karl S. and Buchmann, Stephen L. 1985. Aerodynamics of wind pollination in *Simmondsia chinesis* (Link) Schneider. *American Journal of Botany* 72: 530-539.

Cactus Wren Nests and Evaporative Cooling

Ricklefs, Robert E. and Hainsworth, F. Reed. 1969. Temperature regulation in nestling cactus wrens: the nest environment. *The Condor.* 71: 32-37.

Austin, George. 1974. Nesting success of the cactus wren in relation to nest orientation. *The Condor.* 76: 216-217.

The Rain, The Wash, and the Improbable Pool

Saxton, Dean and Saxton, Lucille. 1973. *Legends and Lore of the Papago and Pima Indians.* University of Arizona Press, Tucson, AZ.

Belk, Denton and Cole, Gerald A. 1975. Adaptational biology of desert temporary-pond inhabitants. Neil Hadley (ed.) *Environmental Physiology of Desert Organisms.* Academic Press, Orlando, Fl.

Elder, J.B. 1956. Watering patterns of some desert game animals. *Journal of Wildlife Management.* 20: 368-378.

Cornejo, Dennis. 1982. Night of the spadefoot toad. *Science 82:* (September) 62-65.

Fisher, S.G. and Grimm, N.B. 1985. Hydrologic and material budgets for a small Sonoran Desert watershed during three consecutive cloudbursts. *Journal of Arid Environments* 9: 105-109.

The Island in the Clouds:

Martin, Pat Preciado and Bernal, Louis Carlos. 1983. *Images and Conversations: Mexican-American Recall a Southwestern Past.* University of Arizona Press, Tucson, AZ.

Bowers, Janice E. and McLaughlin, Stefen P. In press, 1986. Flora and vegetation of the Rincon Mountains, Pima County, Arizona. *Desert Plants.*

McLaughlin, Steven P. In press, 1986. A floristic analysis of the Southwestern United States. *Great Basin Naturalist.*

Marshall, Joe T. Jr. 1956. Summer birds of the Rincon Mountains, Saguaro National Monument, Arizona. *The Condor* 58: 81-97.

Philips, Alan; Marshall, Joe; and Monson, Gale 1978. *The Birds of Arizona.* University of Arizona Press, Tucson, AZ.

Emlen, John T. 1974. An urban bird community in Tucson, Arizona: derivation, structure, regulation. *The Condor* 76: 184-197.

Globe-berry, Javelina and Man

Wilson, Edward O. 1984. *Biophilia.* Harvard University Press, Cambridge, MA.

Rose, J.N. 1912. *Tumamoca,* a new genus in the Cucurbitaceae. *Contributions of the U.S. National Herbarium.* 16: 20-21.

Reichenbacher, Frank W. 1985. *Status and Distribution of the Tumamoc Globe-Berry (Tumamoca macdougalii Rose).* F.W. Reichenbacher and Associates, Tucson, AZ.

Sowls, Lyle K. 1984. *The Peccaries.* University of Arizona Press, Tucson, AZ.

Harris, Larry D. 1984. *The Fragmented Forest.* University of Chicago Press, Chicago, IL.

Berry, Wendell. 1971. To the unseeable animal. *Farming; a Hand Book.* Harcourt, Brace and Jovanovich, New York, NY.

Gary Paul Nabhan is Assistant Director of the Desert Botanical Garden in Phoenix, Arizona and was a cofounder of the Native Seeds/SEARCH. He has written *The Desert Smells Like Rain* and *Gathering the Desert* for which he won the 1986 Burroughs Medal for nature writing. Dr. Nabhan received his PhD in arid lands resources from the University of Arizona and, with his wife, botanist Karen Reichhardt, he was done extensive plant exploration and ecological study in the U.S. and Mexican deserts.